Good Night and Good Sports

BILL ETHERTON

To: Bruce 3/12/16

A great teammate

A mentor who started it all

MHS was

Great in '48!

With Bruce's help/guidance

I tried to make it!

Bill Etherton

ISBN: 1522964371
ISBN-13: 978-1522964377

DEDICATION

This book is dedicated to my wonderful wife, Jodie. She has endured my many health problems in recent years. Jodie has gone far and above any vows of "in sickness and in health"- colon cancer, emergency open heart surgery (with five bypasses), a thoracic procedure (to keep my lungs clear of fluids) and a rare e-coli infection from which I almost didn't survive and hospitalized me for three and a half months with a period of rehab after.

Thanks are not really sufficiently appropriate, but my best expression of great appreciation goes to Dr. Michael Fletcher, chief of staff at Hancock Regional Hospital in Greenfield, Indiana. Words fail me here in describing the care and selfless concerns in keeping me here.

Lastly, when I though I had won the "health lottery" four times (setting a record never to be broken), on my

March 12 birthday of this year I won again. I was informed by Dr. Ravichandran, a specialist at St. Vincent Hospital in Indianapolis, that I had to begin dialysis three days a week, for four hours each time, immobilized in a reclining chair which would continue for the rest of my life. But I thank the Lord because I see others less fortunate than me.

To my Jodie, my love is infinite- so yes, my love, this book is for you.

AUTHOR'S NOTE

When I began my career, there was no round-the-clock coverage of sports on ESPN, so the local broadcaster and his team, along with local newspapers were the only way for a sports fan to receive his or her sporting news.

Unfortunately, it was also a time when a person could not document and record every aspect of his or her life on a blog, Facebook, or some other social media site. So many experiences of these reporters and broadcasters have been lost to the ages.

This book is a small attempt to take you back to those days and to recapture some of the moments that otherwise would be forgotten in time. Everything you read is from my 85-year-old memory, and I have done my absolute best to recall everything accurately. I apologize if there are any discrepancies, and be assured that nothing was left our or changed intentionally. My hope

here is only that you will enjoy this trip down memory lane, and then when it is over you will have smiled and maybe even learned a thing or two.

FOREWARD

When I first met Bill, it was for the purpose of set up and production of Sunday Morning Notre Dame Football highlights. I was impressed with his attention to detail.

With my time at a premium, it was necessary that Bill always be prepared. Bill was not only aware of my tight schedule, but had everything ready for me to go! This greatly impressed me, and we had an excellent relationship. Over the period of time, I heard about Bill's activities and involvement in fundraising for the Big Brothers organization. It was no surprise to me that he was doing a great job. Later when I heard about his franchise sales work at Blimpie's Subs and Salads, I knew he would be a real asset to the company. His record of being a top sales person was another of his accomplishments. I have read this book and was very interesting to discover the people he had met, the

contributions he made to the community, and the life experiences he had which he has graciously shared in this book.

You will be interested to learn, every highlight was perfect, except for one of the Notre Dame-Purdue games which you will read about later.

I respect and value Bill's friendship. He was truly one of the greatest sports announcers and voices of his era.

Ara Parseghian

PROLOGUE

1964. Late November. L.A. Coliseum. Beautiful southern California weather. The traditional gridiron battle between the Fighting Irish of Notre Dame and the Trojans of Southern California.

Today is not the "ordinary" meeting between the two. Notre Dame finds itself under first-year coach Ara Parseghian is unbeaten after after several losing Irish seasons, capped by a 2-6 record the previous year. The very successful and talented Parseghian has guided the Irish to this incredible year's winning record, and a Notre Dame victory would give them not only their first winning record since 1958, but also their first unbeaten year since 1953.

The Irish, led by quarterback John Huarte who would later be awarded the coveted Heisman Trophy, are on top by a score of 17-13. Southern Cal has the ball on the Notre Dame fifteen-yard line and quarterback Craig

Fertig, the USC quarterback, is facing fourth down and eight. The clock is winding down and any possible national championship is on the line. Fertig stars to call signals and...

The best is yet to be. Come join me and the wonderful, treasured memories from my association as radio and TV play-by-play announcer of Notre Dame football and basketball. I will share with you, to the best of my recollection, moments that will allow you to meet some great people in sports who have, over fifteen years, made indelible impressions in my life!

THE BEGINNING OF IT ALL

My ambition to become a sports announcer began as a speech student at Mishawaka High school, a town adjacent to the home of the University of Notre Dame. I would listen to the famous broadcasters of that time in the 1940s – Bill Stern, Ted Husing, and Mel Allen were three of my favorites. Stern and Husing were known for their college football broadcasts and Allen for his baseball coverage of the New York Yankees.

When I was a freshman at Mishawaka High School I ran track, but soon I had to drop all sports to go to work. Like many families, we needed the money, so I worked after school at the Dodge plant from four to eight and then on Saturday mornings as well. But even though I wasn't playing sports, they remained an integral part of my life. I continued to listen to my favorite broadcasters and began to emulate them on my own.

When I had free time, I would go down to a

Mishawaka park and practice announcing games. You could find me sitting on a picnic table and conjuring up match-ups with great detail. "This is Bill Etherton coming to you live from the Rose Bowl in beautiful Pasadena, California." Sometimes I would work in plays that I had heard in the previous weeks, but many times I just let my imagination run wild. It was a good thing no one ever saw or heard me. Of course, later, when I was announcing games for real, I had to remember that I wasn't just imagining it.

A South Bend radio station had a program of various area high school reporters and I was selected as the Mishawaka High representative. Each school was given five minutes to read the high school report that he or she had put together. The program introduced me to a "live" microphone, away from my imaginary practices, and was truly a unique experience because I was "on the air".

When I was a senior, I had won the local American Legion oratorical contest and placed third in the state as well. These successes were important because they helped me receive the Dodge scholarship. So, after graduation I went to Wabash College in Crawfordsville, Indiana, where I majored in speech and English with the intention of becoming a broadcaster.

During my first week at Wabash College, the administrative assistant to the Wabash president contacted me about a possible sports announcer job at the local radio station WFMU. The current sports announcer was being recalled into the army during the Korean war. He was also the sports editor of the local newspaper, the Crawfordsville Journal and Review. Since the newspaper owned the radio station, they were the ones conducting the competitive auditions. Several upper classmen and myself were given a tryout. I was so nervous, and wanted the job so badly, that as I read the copy, my hand shook so much I had to grab it with both hands. The Wabash administrative assistant, Ed Gullion, took us to and from the station as a group in the college van, and when we returned, he asked me to wait until the rest had left. He then informed me that they had selected me. The job was mine if I wanted it! Hallelujah! I said a prayer of thanks and expressed my appreciation to him and started my new job as WFMU sports director the next day.

The high school and college football season was about to start, and it dawned on me that I had the job I always dreamed of having, but I didn't know how to do it.

An alumnus of Notre Dame, Joe Boland, was working for WSBT in South Bend. He was doing all of

their sports coverage and had organized a Notre Dame football radio network. I called Joe and asked him about the pure mechanics for his broadcasts. This wonderful gentleman spent several hours teaching me the how and what of broadcasting football. He was so comprehensive in sparing me nothing but a complete evaluation of his process and procedures. I am still indebted to him for his contributions in getting me off to a great start in announcing play-by-play of football. Later he tragically died of a heart attack while covering a regional high school basketball tournament.

While I was at Wabash College and announcing Wabash football games on WFMU radio

something happened which gave me encouragement to pursue my broadcasting career.

One Sunday morning I was going to a local coffee shop, when an operator of a service station stopped me and gave me a business card. He said a customer Saturday afternoon had heard me doing the Wabash football game, asked if he knew who I was. When the owner said yes, the man gave him his business card and asked him to have me call. I looked at the card. Wow! The man was from WIBC in Indianapolis! Big time radio! Here I am, an eighteen-year-old freshman at Wabash College, being asked to contact a professional broadcaster.

Obviously I called and was invited down to be interviewed. As I recall, he and his program director explained that they were looking for a sports director, and the general manager, Kenneth Church, had been very impressed with my play-by play of the game. I borrowed a sport coat, and took the bus to Indy.

When I got there, I knew at once they had not anticipated a young college freshman. The interview went well, but I knew they were not going to hire someone like me. They said they would get back to me - and later they did call to advise me that they had filled the position. One of their long-time salesmen got the job. You may recognize his name as one of the all-time great 500-mile radio voices – Sid Collins!

I used to see him at some of the Indianapolis sporting events – Butler, IU, Purdue, and Notre Dame basketball games and broadcasters' dinners. I constantly reminded Sid about my WIBC interview and we would talk and joke about switching jobs. Over the years we both even interviewed each other at certain sports games and events.

While working these football games, I attempted to improve my technique and style. One of my most beneficial methods was to study synonyms and work on varying my descriptions, i.e. tackles, stopped, jammed,

hit, went nowhere – creating speech expressions which were shorter and simpler for listeners to follow. I remembered to always give the score and time frequently and to check and confirm the correct pronunciation of players' names. This sounds trivial, but South Bend was and is a very ethnic area. Therefore, I did not have much trouble pronouncing the St. Joseph county players' names which could have been a real problem. Names like Pienesksviell, Vaziak, and Rutzkowski – not many Smiths or Jones. This was really helpful as I pursued my radio and television career in South Bend.

I felt very comfortable with myself in the football broadcast booth, but we also did the broadcasts for Wabash College basketball games, and the high school games for Ladoga, New Market, Linden, Waynetown, and other area schools. I found I had to really get in tune with basketball.

The first game I did at Wingate High School was a disaster. From the get-go everything felt different from a football broadcast. The gym was as small as a "matchbox." The ceiling was so low that anything but a semi-line drive shot would ricochet off the ceiling. We sat at a court-side table instead of high up in the stands. To compound matters worse, we got there late and my prep time was minimal. I was completely lost in the play-by-play. Everything was bang-bang-bang and I didn't have time to get my thoughts together. I really was bad. Very bad. Ag Vance, one of the station owners, was kind in his criticism, but told me I had to get better, and I did. But that first one was a really really bad experience for me and the listeners.

After that experience I began to memorize all the names and numbers before the games, and I did this with no problem. I discovered I had the ability to retain the players' information. Once that happened, the rhythm and flow of the game came more easily. I paid attention to the crowd and was able to use their reactions to accentuate the broadcast, but I also made sure that I didn't fall behind my calls because of the crowd noise. As my experience grew, I tried to develop expression and a style. I continued to rely on my study of synonyms. I researched all the possible words that I could use so that my call and phrases did not become redundant. I also listened and critiqued my tapes frequently. I must have improved well enough because later in the season Ag Vance suggested I submit an audition tape of my work for a chance to broadcast the state finals. I was chosen, over six other announcers, by a select committee of seven Indiana FM stations to do the basketball state finals on the network.

I actually came close to flunking out of college my first year because I was putting in forty to forty-five hours a week at the station. The dean called me in and gave me a lecture about getting my grades up. Luckily, I did and during that summer I worked nights at the station covering activities as the sports editor of the newspaper – the Crawfordsville Journal Review. The time was idyllic and rewarding.

These years at Wabash College and WFMU, laid the groundwork for my career at Notre Dame.

THE EARLY YEARS

Back in the early 1950s, when I started working at WHOT in South Bend, I was the late-night DJ. The station sign-off was at midnight with the national anthem being played. That summer South Bend had a women's baseball team called the South Bend Blue Sox. Many of these women had jobs in the cities where they lived, but a few stayed and worked in South Bend at a Gilbert's Men's Store, which was an operation with a great reputation and served all of northern Indiana and southern Michigan. They were famous for their quality clothing and service. Bonnie Baker was one of the most popular players and a very attractive lady who worked at Gilbert's.

WHOT's sports announcer would broadcast the games on a delay. This was before magnetic audio tapes, and the engineer on duty would record the broadcast on an acetate disc with a needle/stylus cutting out sound grooves similar to vinyl records. Most of you know one

downfall of a vinyl record is that the needle can occasionally get stuck and skip, replaying the same part of the song over and over.

This particular night our station manager, Bill Spencer, was at a bar several miles away from the station. The bartender had the game on the radio listening to the play-by-play account. Our announcer had Bonnie Baker batting and was describing the action.

"Bonnie Baker at bat – the first pitch low and inside – ball one – here's the second pitch – high and inside – now Bonnie Baker has two balls – Bonnie Baker has two balls – Bonnie Baker has two balls."

Spencer raced back to the station to discover the engineer had gone to the bathroom and accidentally locked himself out of the control room, so the transcription kept playing over and over "Bonnie Baker has two balls." Spencer threw a chair through the control room window, opened the door, and moved the transcription ahead – eliminating Bonnie Baker and her two balls.

Another interesting experience during my time at WHOT was the coverage of the annual St. Joseph County 4H Fair. We had a booth at the fair and did daily broadcasts. A feature of our sponsor, Studebaker U.A.W., was a nightly amateur show with some pretty nice cash prizes - $25 to $50 to the winners each evening, with the finals on Saturday night. The U.A.W. president served as the MC of the program.

Saturday night he took the stage to begin announcing. Someone hadn't checked the microphone and it was "hot" when he touched it. He got a pretty good jolt of electricity. Throughout the show he kept forgetting and would touch it and "pow"! He was shocked repeatedly and became the star of the show as the audience kept waiting for him to forget and touch it again.

That same night we had another issue with equipment which involved me taping the show to replay later that night after we finished our ABC radio network programming. A thunderstorm had come through, but the show went on and was well attended. I finished the taping, took it back to the station, and we started it. But the storm had periodically affected our electricity, so the tape would play normally for a minute or two, then would speed up and sound like the three chipmunks, and then slow down dramatically to, "gooooood ooooold soooooongg". Needless to say we weren't able to play the tape.

BOBBY PLUMP AND MILAN

A striking basketball game still lives in my memory. It is the 1953 Indiana state high school championship game, the epic battle between Milan and Muncie Central. David versus Goliath. Jack in the giant killer. No disrespect to the great team from Muncie Central, because they were, after all, in the final game of the tournament and overwhelming favorites that night to win it all. Tiny Milan, as I remember, suited up only nine players. Muncie had a bench loaded with talent.

This was my first series of play-by-play beginning with the sectionals in South Bend. Exciting, yes. Low-scoring, yes. Nail-biting all through the game. Suspense continued to build and build as one team scored only to be followed by the other. Neither team pulled away to a real margin at any time. Then Milan leader Bobby Plump, guarded by Muncie star Gene Flowers, ran the clock down to a final shot and the rest is history!

Our broadcast location was only about twenty feet

away from where Plump took the final, winning shot. One can only admire and respect the ice-water veins, the poise, and the calm to the end of this Indiana high school basketball star who has now become a Hoosier icon like the incomparable Oscar Robertson and Larry Bird. Plump went on to be an outstanding star at Butler University under legendary coach Tony Hinkle.

A sideline note about the Saturday at Hinkle. The governing Indiana High School Athletic Association handled the press by placing the first row full of radio stations, the second row full of newspaper coverage, the third row of more radio stations, and the fourth row of newspaper sports reporters. They did this in an effort to help us radio broadcasters from sitting so close where we would overlap each other as we describe the action. (It really wasn't too successful, but it was a nice try!) The newspaper sports reporter who was assigned the seat behind us was from the Milan area, and he was a very nice guy. I actually used him for occasional comments during the games. In the final game, there were two semi-finals in the afternoon and final at night, it was fortunate for us that we had him right there behind us and and readily available. "Behind" could also be a key word here. The seats at Hinkle seemed to be at about fourteen inches wide, maybe not small but they sure appeared to

be. Here's the punchline – the man's first name, "Tiny". A nickname to be sure, because tiny he was not. He was at least 300 pounds. I did feel much more comfortable sitting in front of Tiny than behind him or beside him.

My unasked for, but sincere, opinion is that Indiana high school basketball, for which has made the state most famous, has lost it. The introduction of class basketball has limited the drama and the opportunity for the "Milans" to have a shot at the big reward and the knowledge that they are the best of ALL! Our country knows the value of a good underdog story as the highly successful movie Hoosiers, starring Gene Hackman, was based on the Milan championship, and it is one of my favorite movies of all time (along with Rudy) but I admit to being slightly prejudiced.

APPLES

After a few months as the evening to sign-off D.J., I was moved to a mid-day to 6 p.m. shift. In those days, product manufacturers would give their various goods to stations to us in give aways and at WHOT we would get quite a variety. We would get everything from Toni hair products to small AM radios and these always seemed to attract listeners.

One day I got a card from the Michigan Apple Growers Association offering five pound bags of apples for use as a promotional give-away. I signed the reply card, checked the space, and sent it back to them.

A few weeks passed before a semi-truck driver came in to see me one afternoon. Our station was located on the second floor above a cigarette and candy distributor – both owned by the same people. The driver said he had some apples for me, and I remember the Michigan promotion for which I had signed. He started

bringing in my apple order upstairs. He brought in a couple of five pound bags, quickly left, and then returned with a few more. He left and brought more apples and then more apples and then more applies until we had bags of apples everywhere – in every office, stacked in the lobby, anywhere there was space. We had to have him begin unloading the rest downstairs, and they finally had no more room.

Completely amazed at the amount of apples that were filling our building, I asked the driver to see his paperwork. It turns out I had ordered – in the box I checked – half of a semi load of apples! For a time, my co-workers addressed me as "Johnny Appleseed!

LOUIE ARMSTRONG

I am grateful to the Good Lord above for blessing me with opportunities to meet so many wonderful people. A non-athlete, but an individual I will never forget, was the musical icon Louie Armstrong.

When I started at WHOT radio in South Bend, I was assigned a number of tasks- helping in the continuity department, writing commercial copy, working in the traffic department, and doing the scheduling for the announcer as to time and placement of the commercial copy in programs. While working the night shift, cleaning and tidying up the office before locking up and leaving was another of my duties.

I did enjoy being the 4 p.m. to midnight DJ and reading the news and weather. I played a lot of records that comprise some real music history from Frank Sinatra to Glenn Miller to Louis Armstrong.

One day, I found out that Louie Armstrong was

making an appearance at a lake resort in Rochester, Indiana, about fifty miles south of South Bend. I called the owner of the resort at Lake Manitou and he invited me down to do an interview with the great Armstrong. It was a sweltering, humid, hot summer evening with the temperature in the 90s with almost no breeze. My arrangement for the interview was to do it around 11:30 p.m. after his show. My plan was to talk a little with him and have Louie introduce some of his hits that we could use at the station.

Mr. Armstrong came in and was literally dripping with perspiration. His clothes appeared to be soaked. It must have been 95-100 degrees in the dressing room and my engineer and I were also sweating heavily. He said, "Give me a minute to get changed from these wet clothes." He then sat there in his undershirt and boxer briefs and said he was ready for the interview. He asked what could he do for us. We discussed what I proposed- I would have him introduce eight or ten of his records which I would then insert in our broadcast segment.

In those days, our equipment was a bulky audio tape recorder which required an engineer to operate while the announcer conducted the interview. We were already set up and ready, so we started. Unfortunately, just after we started, the bus driver came in and gestured for him to

wind it up. I had barely had a chance to talk to this living legend and now he was going to have to leave. But much to my surprise, Louie waved him away and we continued. Picture this, if you will: the great Louie Armstrong, around midnight, after an exhausting performance in 90-degree heat, sitting in his even hotter dressing room, making his band wait in the bus, just so he could keep his word to do an interview with a small town DJ.

But my bad luck had not been completely averted. About twenty minutes into the interview my engineer tapped me on the shoulder and informed me that tape had not been working. The bad news came at the same time another band member came and told him that it was really late and added, "Please, let's leave." No one had to tell me the show was over and that I had messed up my opportunity to interview one of the greatest musical stars of all time. I started to thank him for his time and patience under very trying circumstances when he asked, "Would you like to do it again?" I cannot adequately describe my reaction. That he would even consider doing the interview again, let alone volunteer the idea himself was unbelievable! The second time he was even better.

The WHOT program with the Louie Armstrong interview and his personal introductions several of his hits, including "A Kiss to Build a Dream On" and "Mack

the Knife" were the talk of the town for quite awhile

I will never forget the great Louie Armstrong and for his consideration, his going above and beyond, and the priceless gift of his time. I have always felt that time is the greatest gift you can give another because your time cannot be replaced.

BILL STARCK III

In the mid-1950s WHOT was purchased by WNDU in South Bend, and my broadcasting career was about to take off like I had never dreamed. I was fortunate to spend many, many years at the station but I was never going to make it alone. Throughout my career at WNDU-TV, I met some great people who played major roles in my life. One of these was Bob Freshley of South Bend. Bob is significant because of the man whom I met through him- Bill Starck III. Bill was soon an integral part of my life, both professionally and personally. He became the statistician for all of the telecasts and broadcasts I did. Bill was in the insurance business in South Bend and because of that he could get away to work the games with me. We are talking about airing 32+ high school football games, the Notre Dame football games, at least 110 basketball games, and don't forget to throw in rugby, soccer, boxing and baseball games.

Someone told me, when I was very young, that I will be very lucky – indeed blessed – if I have two, or even three, real friends over the course of my life. They explained I will find many acquaintances, but few who will always be there for me. Bill was this type of friend. But to be honest, he was even more. You see, I am an only child and my father died when I was six months old. Over the years Bill became the brother I never had. "Brother" Bill was a one and only.

Bill had been a star football halfback at Benton Harbor High School in Michigan. He was fast and therefore earned the nickname "Bullet". He was talented enough to play college football at Purdue. He went in the family insurance business and could schedule his own time.

Bill worked with me on radio and television coverage of Notre Dame football, basketball and high school games as well. He was my broadcast statistician and sometimes color commentator over the 15+ years I worked at WNDU TV/Radio. The totals still surprise me – more than 1500 basketball games and more than 550 football games! And these numbers do not include special events like hockey, rugby, Bengal boxing bouts, parades, pre-game shows, and post game broadcasts. His talents were multiple and his many acerbic color

comments were most memorable.

Bill was an outstanding leader in helping South Bend Mayor Joe Kernan bring the College Football Hall of Fame to South Bend. He was also the long-time president of the Moose Krause Notre Dame Chapter of the College Football Hall of Fame.

Bill chaired an annual fundraiser dinner to provide scholarship awards to area high school students who excelled in academics and athletics. Dinner speakers included celebrities like former Bears coach Mike Ditka and ESPN sports announcer Mike Golic, co-host of the Mike & Mike daily morning program.

Bill was a loyal friend both professionally and personally. He used to remind me, "It's a great gig we have!" He passed away a few years ago, but I'm sure he's up there as the stats man for the Big Coach!

PROLOGUE CONCLUDED

...the Trojan quarterback drops back to pass. The Irish have a heavy rush coming and he has to hurry his pass, but Fertig finds Rod Sherman open deep in the Notre Dame secondary, where Sherman grabs the ball in stride.

Irish defensive back Tony Carey turns to pursue and make the stop, but trips and falls. Sherman gets into the end zone for a Trojan touchdown and the lead. The point after gives Southern Cal a 20-17 win! It is a heart-breaking loss for the Irish, and one that takes them out of consideration for the national championship.

But it was a great year. To rebound from a 2-6 record in '63 to an undefeated season until the final game was a miraculous achievement for the Fighting Irish and their brilliant new coach Ara Parseghian. Once again the proud tradition of Notre Dame football's unique heritage

was on the way back.

"Wake up the echoes cheering her name. Shake down the thunder from the sky!" Those verses will again ring out loud and clear across the college football landscape! Ara Parseghian's first 1964 season is but a portent of things to come.

Yes, folks, you ain't seen nothing yet!

JESS HILL

One memorable event with Bill Starck happened in Los Angeles on one of the USC trips. Invariably Bill would get calls from insurance clients about tickets. Most of the time I was able to get them for him. On this one occasion, he needed four tickets, so I went to Ed "Moose" Krause, the Notre Dame Athletic Director, a great, great guy, and asked him about tickets. He told me that he did not have extra tickets this time. He called Jess Hill, his USC counterpart, who informed Starck that he has some tickets that we could purchase. So Bill and I went over to Hill's office to get the four tickets to the next day's game.

Starck had a special business card with a message on each side. His insurance company was an agency of "The Brotherhood Association of Railroad Employees".

The front side had a logo of a locomotive with the following message, "Good for two on any train anywhere in the U.S. - no reservations needed, anytime." The flip side had this message, "Not good on day trains, not good on any train – good and valid to walk along the outside of the railroad tracks."

After Hill sold us the tickets, Starck said, "Thanks, and I really appreciate this Mr. Hill," and gave him one of the cards with the "free" side up. Hill looked at it and said, "This is really great! My wife and I can go up to Oregon and see our kids any time. This is really great! If you guys need any more tickets just call me." I grabbed Starck, said goodbye, and left before he looked at the other side of the card.

The next day we were outside the stadium about two hours before kickoff, having a soda and hotdog, and I saw Hill coming up behind Starck. Hill had this really big-time scowl on his face. I should mention that Jess Hill was a former USC star lineman – a really huge man. I knew we were in trouble when he walked up and belted Starck on the back. The hot dog and Starck's soda went flying. Bill turned around and saw Hill, and we stood there for a few seconds, not knowing what this large man was going to do to us. Then Hill broke into a laugh, smiled, and told us he had taken the card home and

showed his wife the "free" pass from these "great" guys from Notre Dame. She turned it over, saw the "not good" side and showed her husband that we had pulled one over on him.

Fortunately for us, we all had a good laugh about it.

NORTHWESTERN TRAFFIC

Another memorable time with Bill was a trip to Evanston, Illinois, for a Northwestern-Notre Dame game. (This was when Ara Parseghian was still coaching the Wildcats before being hired at Notre Dame.) There was a high school championship game, the Northern Indiana Title Contest at School Field in South Bend on Friday night before the Saturday Notre Dame game. I planned that we would do the radio broadcast of the high school game Friday night game and drive to Evanston the next morning. Bill agreed he would pick me up with plenty of time to get to the stadium to set up and prepare.

Saturday morning came and he was late – not just late by a small amount of time, but hours late!! Obviously I was pretty nervous the entire trip to Evanston. I knew that the kickoff and the telecast would not wait for us, and I had never missed a broadcast.

On entering Evanston, we soon discovered parking

was blocking half of the streets. This was in contrast to the way South Bend handles Notre Dame traffic on game day which is to temporarily prohibit parking on streets to the stadium and send traffic one way into the stadium area. Quick, efficient and convenient! However, here at Northwestern there were no one-way patterns to ease the flow as in South Bend. It was just normal traffic! I became more and more upset as I constantly checked my watch, which at that time, I just knew was moving too fast! I yelled at Starck to get going, so we started to break all the safe driving rules, and began to make great time, when all of a sudden I saw the biggest motorcycle policeman standing in front of a wooden horse blocking our way. He seemed to be about nine feet tall wearing his high boots, helmet, Ray Ban sunglasses, and a short leather jacket! His arms were crossed, and he stood waiting for us. I knew we were in big time trouble, and that I was going to miss the game, lose my job, and be in jail for one hundred years!

He took his time sauntering up to Starck on the driver's side, so Starck put the window down. If we could have seen through the Ray Bans, I would tell you he was glaring at us and getting ready to explode. At this moment Starck came up with one of the greatest lines ever spoken. Before the officer could begin to rip us apart, Starck said, “Officer, am I glad to see you!” The policeman was stunned. Starck continued before he could recover and said, “Do you want me to slow down and move over? We are from WNDU-TV in South Bend. I have to do the telecast of today's game.” The cop was completely off balance with Bill's question.

We got a brief lecture about leaving earlier to do the game. When the officer finished with his lecture, without giving us a ticket, Starck very seriously said, “Do you want us to drive more carefully and obey the rules when we leave?” The officer responded with, “Why the hell would you do that now? I should run you in, but get the hell out of here and don't hurt anyone.” About a half mile down the road, we ran into another road block, but Starck told them that Officer Jones had cleared us and they let us go. We made the game, but Ara beat us handily – again. Father Joyce hired him after that season ended and the rest is history.

CAR RUNNING IN MIAMI

There are experiences in our lives that remind us periodically to be a little more humble. This lesson, although not a really big deal, is a good example. It happened when Notre Dame played Miami in the old Orange Bowl stadium.

Bill Starck and I had a good friend, Bob Freshley, the man who had introduced us, who drove us from the hotel to the stadium in Bob's new car, a Cadillac convertible with a white top and blue body. The car had a Michigan license plate.

The game was underway when in the middle of the first quarter during a time out, the public address announcer said, "Attention, please. There is a white and blue Cadillac convertible with Michigan license plates, whose doors are locked, and your engine is running!"

I looked over at Freshley and he shook his head, pulled the car keys out of his pocket, and held them up so

Starck and I could see them. Not our car! Who was the dummy from Michigan with a car like ours who locked his or her car with the engine running! Ho! Ho! Ho!

The P.A. announcer repeated the message several more times. Each announcement drew more laughs from us. We had our car keys. The keys were not left in the ignition in our car.

The game ended and we went down to pick up our car and guess what? It was our car and we were the dummies whose car was still running with an eighth of a tank showing on the fuel gauge. When Freshley parked and turned the key off, it left the ignition stuck in the on position. We had the keys, but... So the lesson was, and is, be humble. Don't laugh too much about "others mistakes!" The joke may be on you!

PITTSBURGH FLIGHT

One lesson I learned the hard way occurred on an Friday afternoon flight from South Bend to Pittsburgh to cover the Irish-Panther football telecast the next day.

On this occasion, I didn't fly with the team, but flew in a private plane owned by one of our sponsors who was involved in the Elkhart, Indiana, mobile home business and who also owned a sports bar in South Bend.

I had lunch with him and two of his business associates, and then the four of us went to the airport, got in the plane, a Bonanza, and left for Pittsburgh. We all had a lot of coffee at lunch and we had Cokes and snacks on the plane.

On a small private plane there are no restrooms. To be bluntly descriptive, large bottles are the generally restrooms on long flights.

After awhile, the coffee started to catch up with me. I managed to tell myself we would be in Pittsburgh soon and I didn't want to use the container. The urge grew strong and stronger and I thought another Coke would help in some way, dumb, dumb, and dumber! I was not in dire straits, but getting there. Then I looked out the window and saw a large number of lights – we are here finally, I thought. I asked my friend, the pilot, how soon we would be landing. His answer was "about another hour!" The city I saw below us was Akron, Ohio. "My, oh my!" was all I could say. The next hour was pure, unadulterated torture.

As soon as we taxied to a halt and finally landed in Pittsburgh, I must have been jet propelled as I jumped out of the plane and hurried as fast as I could on the tarmac toward the terminal building and their restrooms. I could not straighten up – I was doubled over.

At that time, in the movies there were four brothers that were comedians, called the Marx Brothers – one of them was named Groucho and he was famous for three things – his constant smoking of cigars, his bushy mustache, and his distinctive walk – always bent over. As I darted across the tarmac, I must have resembled this famous comedian, because I heard several other arrivals say, "Isn't that Groucho Marx almost running to the terminal?" I was forced to imitate Groucho (without the cigar or the mustache!)

I don't mean to be gross, but it seemed like hours before my bladder and I became more "pleasant" to each other.

Aviation rule for passengers and the pilot – watch your liquids before your flight!

SHERM SEARER

From the very beginning of my career at WNDU TV/radio, I was always searching for ways to make my television reporting something more special and different from my competitors – to make my sports coverage so good that each night, "You wouldn't want to miss anything on Channel 16 sports!" as their tagline would remind the viewers.

I met a man from Elkhart, Indiana, Sherm Searer, at a service club luncheon where I was giving a talk on our sports coverage and what we did at WNDU to constantly improve and enhance our sports programming.

Sherm had been a fighter pilot in WWII – flying the fastest fighter plane at that time – a P-38 Lightning. This, along with the P-51 Mustang, were the most famous and deadly of all the U.S. planes. He flew countless missions without a scratch. We talked at length about planes and he explained to me about a major early glitch with the P38. In the beginning, both engines cycled the same way producing a cavitation into one direction. It was a deadly

error for many pilots and it was necessary to solve the problem. The dilemma was solved by counter rotating each propeller in opposite directions.

He told me he was a pilot with two small planes – a Mooney Mark 21 and a twin engine Beechcraft plane. Sherm was also a Bardall engine additive distributor. We discussed an advertising trade-out in exchange for flying me to various sports locations. This would allow us to get breaking news on the air sooner. It sounded great to me, and I went back and outlined my plan to our station manager. I got the go ahead, and it opened a big, wide world of possibilities for me. Low and behold here was a local TV station with hot, breaking news and interviews on the air that same night!

Sherm flew Chuck Linster, our WNDU Chief photographer, and I to the College All-Stars football team practices in a suburb of Chicago to do interviews and get them on the air that night. (This was a few years ago when the Chicago Tribune sponsored a charity football game at Soldier Field, between the college all-stars and NFL champions.)

Also, we flew to Mohammed Ali's headquarters for his bout with Sonny Liston. We flew to interview jockey Bill Hartfak as he prepared for the Kentucky Derby. We visited the Indy 500 practices and qualifications seeing

Parnelli Jones set the 160 mph record. We interviewed tennis stars Jimmy Conners and Billie Jean King at the Indianapolis Open tennis tournament. We acquired the reputation of being first with breaking news involving sports celebrities and events.

Our radio station also carried regular season Chicago White Sox baseball games. So I contacted their Chicago office and offered them a proposition - one they couldn't afford to refuse! Sherm Searer had made the twin engine Beechcraft available for longer flights and it was a perfect opportunity to expand our coverage beyond the regular season and drum up interest in the team during spring training. Remember, this was before ESPN and round-the-clock-sports coverage. Most people had no way to get first-hand information on events that were not happening locally.

The Chicago White Sox team did their spring training in Sarasota, Florida. They owned a hotel there and a couple of small restaurants (one of them was almost a duplication of what we have today come to know as "Subway" with great deli sandwiches and sides like potato salad and baked beans.) I suggested that right after the Indiana High School Basketball Tournament finals that I would fly down to Sarasota for a week, stay at their facilities, and do White Sox player interviews as well

as ones with the visiting teams' members. We also intended to fly to other Florida cities such as Bradenton, Fort Myers, Tampa, Fort Lauderdale and record as many interviews as time would permit. The club accepted the proposal and off we went.

Our interviews that year included Mickey Mantle, Stan Musial, Willie Mays and Phil Rizzuto. I assembled a file of interviews I could use when appropriate during the season's broadcasts. For example, I did one with Roger Maris of the Yankees so on that day later in the year when he set the home run record, I could pull his comments made earlier at Fort Lauderdale which added perspective to the momentous event. These interviews gave my sports programs that priceless asset of immediacy and individual flair. The Sox were ecstatic about it. It was a great marketing and promotion for them and for us, and would never have been possible without Sherm.

Sherm Searer was one of the truly outstanding people I ever met. We maintained a friendship over the years, but, as often happens, our contact lessened as time went on. Years later, I was in Indianapolis when I found out that Sherm had been severely injured in an auto accident as a result of someone running a red light. His injury was extensive, but he did recover. The irony of this situation was he flew countless missions in World War II

without a scratch and here at home a tragic crash impaired his ability to ever fly again.

WJIM OFFER

When I was doing all of the Notre Dame games at WNDU-TV, I got a call from Hal Gross, the owner of the station at WJIM-TV East Lansing, Michigan, the sports outlet for Michigan State football and basketball. He inquired if I was available to talk about their sports play-by-play and sports director position. I didn't reply at once. I talked to my friend, Bill Starck, about it. He said I should go up, listen to what they might offer because, "What could I lose by doing it?!"

I made the appointment and Starck drove us to East Lansing. The interview was going well I thought – and then the owner asked me if I could ad-lib a game play-by-play. We went into a studio and improvised a Notre Dame-Michigan State football game. It was easy for me, and, of course, I had the Irish ahead 35-7 by the end of the first quarter. Mr. Gross stopped me there, said that was sufficient, and asked me to sit and discuss what I needed

to come to work there. And then Starck said he would negotiate for me and that he was my business agent! We went back to Mr. Gross's office.

Starck told the owner, what I needed as a start - $50,000 a year, a new car, an expense account, money for a clothing allowance, a membership to the country club, and a substantial talent fee for the games.

I sat there in the office in shock when I heard what he proposed! No one was crazy enough to accept that package! The owner said he would consider it, discuss it with his program director, and let me know in a few days.

True to his word, he did, and said he was interested. He wanted to know if I would come back and talk more about the terms and told me if I could compromise on a couple of the items, we would have a deal.

By this time, I realized that Bill didn't want me to leave, and these "incredible" demands had been his way of keeping me there. And fortunately, I was happy to have the job of a lifetime, so I told him thanks for the offer – but no thanks!

ROCKY BLEIR

One of my most treasured and memorable events occurred during a Notre Dame football season. Everyone should have the opportunity to attend a Notre Dame home game. The pre-game festivities outside the stadium and the preliminaries on the field before kick-off are – in my mind – without equal!

When the anthem is about to be played a certain ceremony takes place. An honored celebrity carries the colors around the field from the Notre Dame dugout on the west side of the field, across the fifty-yard line to the flag pole at the extreme north east location. "America the Beautiful" is played on the walk carrying the flag to the resplendently uniformed Irish Guards. It is quite a moment – the guards raise the flag as the "Star Spangled Banner" is played.

A Notre Dame football captain who had graduated and served in Vietnam was the individual honored this

particular Saturday. He had been severely wounded in Vietnam when a mine destroyed a major portion of his foot. Doctors had told him he would never walk normally again. He carried the colors across the field – hobbling on his cane.

It was one of the most heart-wrenching, but uplifting moments in my lifetime!

But the end of the story is unforgettable – almost a movie fiction – because the young man who had been given the word about never walking normally again was Rocky Bleir of the four-time Super Bowl champion Pittsburgh Steelers and teammate of Terry Bradshaw, quarterback; Franco Harris, tailback; Mean Joe Green, Hall of Fame tackle and the star of the great Coca-Cola commercial. The man who beat the odds – Rocky Bleir!!

PURDUE GAME

The Purdue-Notre Dame games were always a fantastic rivalry. Games with the Boilermakers coach, Jack Mollenkopf, and Ara Parseghian of Notre Dame were always close and exciting and did not always end with the Irish winning. This particular year both teams were unbeaten and the game was scheduled for Ross-Ade Stadium in West Lafayette. There was a sell-out wherever the game was played. We wanted to televise the game live.

The Purdue athletic director, Red Mackey, was an outstanding gentleman and a good friend of Ed "Moose" Krause, his Notre Dame counterpart. However, our presentation to air the game live fell on deaf ears. Mackey would not allow a live telecast even though the game had been a sell-out from the beginning of the season. The fact that both teams were unbeaten made it even more desirable. But Mackey was adamant, and he was the authority, the man.

I suggested to our station management that we contact him with the idea of filming it and showing it on a delay later that evening. They thought it was a good idea, and I thought Mackey would allow it. He did agree and everyone was happy.

I called a camera company in Chicago and arranged for our chief photographer, Chuck Linster, to go and get a special camera with extra large film capacity so we wouldn't break down or interrupt the flow of plays. The police department in West Lafayette agreed to pick us up right after the game and get us to the airport where our plane was waiting. We had to fly back to South Bend to get the film developed and on the air by 8 p.m. The South Bend police would pick us up and rush us to the station. Everything went like clock-work. Ara and I set up in the studio to narrate the game. A lot of his team came into the studio and got down on the floor to watch the program. We had promoted the telecast heavily saturating the air with promos Thursday and Friday so the potential viewership was huge! I began the telecast with the usual introductions of Ara and myself and asked him for some opening comments to set the stage. Then we broke for commercials. Here I should tell you that every Sunday morning I would edit the game film of Saturday's game for

the Notre Dame highlights show. Ara would come in later in the day around noon and we then taped the hour-long program. As a result, we had a pretty good working television relationship since I also had done a live play-by-play of almost every game except for the few that were covered on a national network.

I began to describe the kickoff and return. As we started the re-play, we saw a shot of the sky, the stands, but no game. I set up the next play, but again wild shots of blue sky and the crowd. Ara looked at me with a, "What's going on!" I got a cue from the floor director to do a break for commercials. Ara was very upset, as was I. The telephone switchboard was going crazy. Following the commercial break, we tried again – same story – no game shots and again another commercial. We had to pull the film and run an apology for the error. The problem was caused by a lack of coordination between the view finder and the camera lens. Fortunately, we had a multitude of still pictures from the fax machine to use, and Ara and I interviewed many of the players who were in the studio. Big game, big promos, big flop.

Moral of the story is always check your equipment and avoid a big-time error!

A 10-10 TIE!

One of the most unforgettable college football games I ever covered, but did not announce, was the most famous of all time – the Notre Dame-Michigan State game in 1966.

ABC was going to broadcast the Saturday game, and there was also a ND-MSU reserve game on the night before the "Big One". We asked, and received, permission to broadcast the game on WNDU-radio. So Bill Starck and I went up to broadcast the freshman game. The game was played at a high school field. It was attended by one of the largest football crowds to ever go to this kind of contest.

No other radio stations did the game. When we completed setting up our equipment, we were surprised and delighted to discover MSU's Athletic Director, "Biggie" Munn, and his ND counterpart, Moose Krause, were sitting behind us. What a great availability to have them comment on the game and about what was to come on Saturday. It worked out well, their comments throughout our broadcast were priceless, but – and here is the rub – they both smoked cigars so the air was not only difficult to breathe after awhile, and almost too dense to see through to call the game. A nightmare on one hand, but priceless on the other is my description of that event!

The build-up for the big game on Saturday was unprecedented and the national telecast would be seen by (at that time) a record number of viewers. The contest between the two unbeaten teams was played under cold, gray skies before a capacity crowd in East Lansing Spartan Stadium. Their announcers were my friends, nationally famous Chris Schenkel, doing the play-by-play, and former Oklahoma coaching icon, Bud Wilkinson, doing the color commentary.

Bill Starck and I were in a press box to watch so that we would be able to report our comments on the game later on my television program on WNDU. It also was important to me to make notes for when I would be editing the game highlights for our regular Sunday program. I mention the ABC coverage because the sound was available in our booth and supplemented some material we might have missed.

Since I was only covering the game, and not

announcing it, I could sit back, watch, and yell as much as I wanted to. This was quite the contrast from when I was announcing Notre Dame games either on TV or radio. Normally I had to remain focused and somewhat impartial, so this game Starck and I had a field day venting our full emotions. Incidentally, Michigan Governor George Romney sat in the booth next to us.

The game was full of mind-boggling hitting on both sides – several players were injured fairly early in the game, including the Irish quarterback Terry Hanratty, who left the game with an injured shoulder. Many of the players on both teams went on to play in the National Football League. Michigan State's great defensive star, Bubba Smith and George Webster are the two Spartans I remember the most. Notre Dame's Jim Lynch, George Goeddeke, Jim Seymour and Nick Eddy also became outstanding professionals.

The scoring was tough to come by for both teams that day and Notre Dame was able to tie it 10-10 at the top of the fourth quarter, but a failed missed field goal by the Irish later in the quarter kept the score the same when Notre Dame received a Michigan State punt with just over three minutes left in the game. At this point coach Parseghian chooses to run the ball, hoping to break one for the distance and score, but most vital, he does it to

maintain possession of the ball. Why doesn't he open it up and try to throw? Irish quarterback Coley O'Brien, is diabetic and tiring rapidly. On a previous series, his passes were wobbly and no where close to the intended receiver. Therefore, not wanting to risk a fatal turnover, Ara keeps the ball on the ground and, thus, keeps control of the game.

The game ends 10-10 and the critics initiate the controversial uproar- the Notre Dame Fighting Irish played for the tie! The sports world of anti-Irish went berserk! And to this day coach Parseghian is criticized for his decision. However, Duffy Daugherty's Spartans had the ball near midfield on the series before, and he chose to also play it conservatively when he had three downs in which he could have passed to try to score. He ended up punting to the Irish. And don't forget that he was working with an outstanding and very healthy quarterback by the name of Jimmy Raye.

Let me also remind you that Notre Dame, with a healthy quarterback, went on to beat Southern California 59-0 the next week, which allowed them to win a National Championship.

I will always remember this game but not because of the tie. I'll remember it more because of the strategy and football moves in this game were another example of

the genius of one of the greatest gridiron coaches of all time – Notre Dame icon Ara Parseghian. I feel truly honored to have worked with and to know the great coach and the gracious gentleman he has always been.

HOCKEY GAME

The University of Notre Dame had a hockey "club" when I was there, not a hockey varsity team. Soccer and rugby were among the other "clubs" whose sports were telecast. I really enjoyed looking into what each of these sports had to offer and how they pushed me as an announcer.

One year there was a hockey game with the Irish facing off against an opponent whom I can't recall– but that doesn't really matter in my "adventure" to become a "premier hockey announcer."

South Bend, Indiana, is a wonderful city in which to live – if you like cold. And I mean very cold and lots of that white stuff! So picture, if you will, an outdoor hockey rink in Howard Park in South Bend. That "South" is misleading because it stands for the south bend in the St. Joseph River – not down south with warm temperatures. There is a city in southern Indiana by the name of North

Vernon. Geographically, names are misleading.

Bill Starck and I dressed as well as we could considering how frigid the day would be for us. We would be outside attempting to talk in a smooth manner reflecting that the extreme cold didn't bother us.

I asked the Notre Dame assistant basketball coach, Larry Staverman, if I could interview him during the break between the first and second periods of the hockey game. So the game simulcast was set up as I planned.

The game started and I was a little behind in my initial play-by-play of the contest, but I fell into a rhythm shortly and felt that I was on top of things with my descriptions.

The break came and Coach Staverman – all 6'8" of him and me at 5'8" – walked out on the ice for our interview. The first few minutes went well and then the cold of the ice penetrated my leather shoe soles. I had worn a heavy jacket, pants and long underwear, but I overlooked the most important item – boots! But after the cold became more and more and more chilling, my feet reminded me I had no boots. As I held the microphone up so Staverman, at 6'8", could answer my questions, I couldn't stop my hand holding the mike from shaking. So I grabbed it with both hands, and I shook even more. Larry reached over to steady it, and he did for a short

minute. Then the cold hit him, and the mike started to shake even more. Larry put his other hand over our hands and the mike! We were like Mutt and Jeff doing the interview! Our combined grip didn't do the job very long and there we stood, in the center of the rink, unable to keep the mike from shaking like a willow tree on a windy summer day. Mutt and Jeff freezing – the director, whom I could hear chuckling in my headset, asked if I would like to end our interview and come up in the stands where they had a portable heater. We were up there in a heartbeat. We closed our spectacular hockey interview and raced to the stands.

To indicate how cold it was that day – the concession stand was about thirty feet from our simulcast location. They sent us over coffee and it froze before it got to us!

WASPS and GOLF

One year we decided to expand our summer sports coverage by televising the annual member-guest golf outing at the South Bend Country Club. The club had a wonderful professional, a delightful character by the name of John Watson. He had a delightful Scottish brogue and always had a funny anecdote about golf's big names- Sam Snead, Byron Nelson, Tommy Bolt, and others. John Watson and I took the position of anchoring our telecast and he was magnificent with his analysis of the members and guests play.

While we were prepping for the telecast, I squatted down by the scorer's registration table to get some information. Suddenly, I had this terrible needle-like piercing pain in my upper right thigh. I straightened up, and as I did a dead wasp dropped out of my slacks and fell on the ground. I started to have trouble standing and unfortunately had a severe reaction to the wasp sting. Several of the people took me to the club house and its locker room where I laid down and was treated. Here is where I was fortunate. The golf tournament had a multitude of doctors around. Several of them attended to me. We still had an hour until air time and I was alright to begin. If something had to happen, I was in the right place at the right time with an army of doctors around to handle any medical problem.

Later that year, my friend Sherm Searer and I flew to Indianapolis where they were playing in a golf tournament to get some interviews. I met the icon Sammy Snead, Tommy Bolt, a U.S. Open champion, and Charlie Sifford, who was one of the top pros at that time.

Snead, to my surprise, was difficult to talk to, limited our time to talk, and in general was very condescending. Charlie Sifford, however, was one of the friendliest in the professional ranks and could not have been more cooperative. He puffed constantly on a cigar while we talked and demonstrated various golf shots for us. He was truly an outstanding gentleman.

Tommy Bolt had the reputation of a ferocious temperament and Watson had said to hope for a good day with him. Fortunately, he was very considerate, talked

freely about his temper, and was a great interview.

To my regret, I never did get to interview Byron Nelson, Jack Nicklaus, or Arnold Palmer.

JOHN JORDAN, CHESTY CHIPS, and NOTRE DAME BASKETBALL

When I started doing play-by-play of Notre Dame basketball games, I met one of the most unforgettable people of my career. His name was John Jordan, an Irish man through and through, who was a Notre Dame graduate and an outstanding coach.

Bill Starck and I would be invited up to Coach Jordan's room after a game on the road and together, with the team's chaplain, Father Tom Brennan, we would critique the game.

Father Brennan was also the custodian of the original cabin in which the University's founder, Father Sorin lived in 1842. (Father Brennan was a great handball player who used to beat almost everyone including most of the football coaches.)

All in all, it was a wonderful experience to share

this time – win or lose, (winning was much better!) with these three outstanding people over an adult beverage. These too were truly unforgettable times. We were able to witness and discuss many great players over the years such as, Mike Graney and Bob Bradke from Hammond, Indiana; Tom Hawkins, who later worked on Los Angeles Radio; Junior Stephens; Gene Duffy; Ron Reed, from LaPorte, Indiana, who later was star baseball pitcher with the Atlanta Braves. We even saw a couple of football players who tried their ability on the hardwood. All-American quarterback and Heisman Trophy winner Paul Hornung, who was a 6'4" 220 pounder, and All-American pro defensive tackle Kevin Hardy who was 6'6" and 220 pounds. My memory recalls they both rebounded with "authority". And I shouldn't forget to mention Walt Sahm from Indianapolis, who was a very talented center and a vital member of the Irish basketball team.

One of the key sponsors of Notre Dame basketball games was Chesty Potato Chips. They were big in Indiana sports coverage - a major sponsor of Indiana University, Purdue University and Butler. Our home games were simulcast with my radio play-by-play on TV as well. Chesty got a great double buy with the two for one coverage.

Chesty was one of the few sponsors who gave a

great deal of latitude and freedom to the presentation of the commercials by the announcer. If I thought an ad-lib or spontaneous comment was appropriate to make that particular bag of chips more effective, they encouraged it.

Our broadcast location in the old Notre Dame field house was right above the top row of the student bleachers. Some of the football players would sit in that top row. A couple of players I knew pretty well were in this top row the night of our first game being sponsored by Chesty. They were Monte Stickles and George Izo, who both went into the NFL. Stickles, I understand, later became a San Francisco radio personality.

Chesty gave a lot of bags of chips as props to use on some of their commercials – traditional, garlic, extra garlic, barbecue, and others. Our first commercials were for the extra garlic chips. I handed some bags of chips to the two footballers who were sitting right below us. "Try these Chesty Chips guys (they had some – actually a lot.) I leaned over with the microphone to get their response and received great enthusiasm and comments about the chips, but also an overwhelming dose of extra garlic breath! We talked briefly about the great taste but the garlic fumes almost took my breath away! The breeze from the extra garlic – WOW! Almost too, too, much. I learned a lesson there and never forgot it. Always check

the product thoroughly and then check it again! Fortunately, my lungs cleared and my throat and I went on with my description of the game.

The next day one of the Chesty advertising agency account people, who had checked and watched our simulcast, called our station manager, Bernie Barth, and raved about our presentation. I got an "atta boy" for this, my choice of Chesty Chips, and a nice letter from that rep who had monitored the game and who was responsible for the compliment.

Another interesting incident took place one year at the Notre Dame-DePaul basketball series. The Irish, under Johnny Jordan, were in the middle of a great season when DePaul came to Notre Dame to play in the old Notre Dame field house. There were a limited number of seats for the visitors and since DePaul had an outstanding team also, they had many of their fans that were unable to get tickets. DePaul lost this very close game, and to compound the frustration of losing, they felt they had been shorted on visitors' ticket allotment.

Later that season we had a date to play them in Chicago. It was a sellout and they limited us in the number of visitor's tickets.

As often was the case, some of Bill Starck's insurance clients called him at the last minute for tickets

to the game. We could not get any from DePaul, although I tried. Bill felt very obligated to these particular clients, so I improvised.

There were four clients looking for tickets, and the broadcast seating was for three people. I did the engineer's job on our broadcasts, so we had one vacant seat to use – that left three we had to take care of.

That night at the gate I had one of the men carry a screwdriver and a pair of pliers (to pose as an equipment tech), the second client carried two microphones (another equipment tech), and the third carried a piece of equipment in our carrying case. Bill and I wore our WNDU radio blazers and necessary credentials. I told the ticket taker these gentlemen were part of our "broadcast team".

We went down to our broadcast seats and table. The DePaul sports publicity director saw my entourage and came running over. He was upset, there was a lot of pressure on him that night, and yelled, "What am I going to do with them – no seats!" I asked him if they could sit on the floor beside us and added, "Could they please stay?"

He reminded me of their unhappy treatment at South Bend. Finally, he calmed down and I told him I would make it up to him if he would allow me this favor.

He did, and picture this – a jam packed arena and three avid fans sitting on the floor at the press table in front of us.

Never before and never again did I put myself in that kind of a situation. They owed Starck a really big one after this. I returned the favor to the DePaul sports publicity director with dinner in a South Bend restaurant and a seat in my announcing booth at a later Notre Dame football game.

JOHN WOODEN

One of the legendary sports figures I had always wanted to meet was the great John Wooden of UCLA. Wooden's NCAA basketball championship record is one that will never be equaled or broken. Ten championship titles were won by UCLA during his coaching career.

Bill Starck and I annually would finish our high school championship game broadcast and hustle over to a restaurant near Hinkle Field House for a late dinner before heading back to South Bend. The restaurant television almost always was showing the NCAA finals and UCLA seemed to be playing some one each year for the title. We mused about the plays displayed by UCLA and the strategy employed by Wooden. We discussed his South Bend background and wondered what he was like off the court as well as on.

We talked about the hope that some day UCLA would be playing in Chicago Stadium as part of a double

header involving Notre Dame, and we would have an opportunity to meet and interview him. Wooden was from Martinsville, Indiana, a great star at Purdue, a former coach at South Bend Central High School and a coach at Indiana State in Terre Haute, before his years at UCLA.

The next year we did play at the stadium and UCLA was in the first game. Our broadcast location was next to the UCLA bench and gave us a fantastic view of Wooden's coaching style and technique throughout their game. There was a hockey rink over which the basketball court was placed so it was a little "chilly" down on or near the court. Wooden had high-top, four-buckle overshoes and extra-large top coat, big scarf and a cap pulled down around his head as far as it would go. He carried with him his signature rolled-up program in his hand which he used to gesture and direct players to various positions on the court.

Bill and I had broadcast many games where we were adjacent to coaches and so many times profanity was routine, but we did not hear one profane remark from John Wooden. The most extreme words we heard from him were "Gol' darn it!" or "Dog gone it!" or "That's a bad call, ref!"

We had a brief period between games and

approached Coach Wooden, introduced ourselves, and asked if he had time for an interview. He apologized and explained that they were leaving for the airport and a flight back to L.A. right away. He was most gracious, and impressed Bill and I as the kind gentleman we had heard and read about.

It is ironic how certain events happen, both unexpected and very pleasing, because that summer I had to speak at a Kiwanis Club luncheon in South Bend and talked briefly with a friend, Walter Kindy, who was a teacher at South Bend Central High School and their athletic ticket manager. Over the course of our conversation, he told me an old friend of his was coming back to Indiana to spend a couple of weeks at their lake cottage just north of South Bend in Michigan. He asked if I would like to meet and maybe do an interview with him. It was coach John Wooden and his wife who were Walter's friends!

Some events are truly amazing when they occur, and this is one of my most memorable ones!

Coach Wooden offered several thoughts during our visit –

- Never set a goal you can't attain
- But always establish a goal which will test

you in its accomplishment

- **Discipline in life is a key factor in being successful**
- **Always play by life's rules**

I asked him about some of his teams and players. He talked about Gail Goodrich and his ability to lead and perform under pressure. He named Lew Alcindor (Kareem Abdul-Jabbar) and Bill Walton as two of his greatest players. Both were centers who had the ability to dominate games. He described Mike Warren, a South Bend Central great, as one of his greatest play-makers. Warren played a major role in Wooden's many NCAA championships. He later had a motion picture career.

He told me a story about Bill Walton, who was a great player but also a very free spirit. At the beginning of one of the basketball seasons, Walton came back to school with extra, extra long hair and when Wooden asked him about it and its appearance, Walton told the coach he had a right to wear his hair any way he chose. Coach Wooden then observed, "Bill, that's correct, but I am the coach of our team and that gives me the right to choose whom I want to play!" Walton cut his hair the next day.

John Wooden was a Hoosier legend, a basketball

icon, and an incomparable leader of men! I have never forgotten this great man and what he called his native Hoosier philosophy of "Kindness and Friendship".

LEE MARVIN, LLOYD BUCHER and RAYMOND BERRY

Another celebrity who remains vividly in my memory is Lee Marvin. I was fortunate to have met him on one of our football trips for I had always admired his work. One of my favorites was The Dirty Dozen, which also featured all-time football great Jim Brown and Telly Savalas. Other credits of Marvin's include Paint Your Wagon and the John Wayne movie The Man Who Shot Liberty Valance. He told me he loved football – followed teams in the NFL more than college, but wanted to talk about USC – ND. I asked him to be on the air with me sometime.

Not many people know that Marvin not only portrayed a soldier in some of his movies, but he had been a marine himself. He was a private first class during World War II and fought in the Pacific theater. He was

wounded at the Pacific battle for Saipain for which he received the Purple Heart. When he finally came on at half time of another game with USC in Los Angeles, I talked to him about his medal and bravery under fire. Marvin thanked me for the kind words, but as many great soldiers do, he deflected the compliment to others with whom he served. After his death he was buried in Arlington National Cemetery.

During a game when Notre Dame was playing at Iowa, I had the honor and privilege of interviewing another former serviceman, Captain Lloyd Bucher of the USS Pueblo, a ship that was captured by North Korean forces during the Vietnam War. It was a very controversial incident at the time because the United States claimed the ship was international waters, not North Korean territory. Regardless, Commander Bucher and his crew were held captive for a prolonged period of time, and Bucher was even tortured physically and mentally. Eventually he and his crew were freed, but the ship remains in North Korean custody to this day. It was obvious that the incident was still troubling for the commander, so we moved on to talk about the game (which we won). Bucher received numerous awards for his service over the years including a Purple Heart. I feel

truly blessed to have had the opportunity to meet him.

There is a lake near Warsaw, Indiana, which was (and may still be) the site for Christian faith meetings held periodically in the summer. Winona Lake is beautiful and frankly, when you visit there, it brings a deep sense of peace and tranquility. I went down to a meeting of the Fellowship of Christian Athletes to obtain some interviews for TV/Radio. Among those to whom I talked with were NFL stars, Raymond Berry, of the then Baltimore Colts, and the legendary icon, Johnny Unitas! They are both Professional Hall of Fame members. When I met Ray Berry, I wasn't speechless, but pretty close. Having watched him get the Colts a win with an "impossible" catch for a touchdown many times, I had visualized perhaps a physical Mr. America-type of person – an S for Superman on his chest. Ray Berry was barely six feet tall, fairly slight, and not an imposing figure at all. He was gracious, humble, and considerate during our visit and made a point of emphasizing his Christian faith. He stressed discipline and goal setting. He told me how he and Unitas would work out and practice by themselves after the regular practice sessions ended. Oh yes, Berry told me he had average speed and that one of his legs was shorter than the other, and that he always had to

wear built-up shoes!

It never ceases to amaze me what I have been able to learn about others and their accomplishments. But I have found that dedication, sacrifice, discipline, and goal setting were the attributes found in almost every coach, player, or celebrity who had accomplished great success.

PAT O'BRIEN

Sometimes in our lives we receive surprises which are as unexpected as they are most pleasant and appreciated. A surprise which happened to me one spring at Notre Dame fell perfectly into that category.

Notre Dame athletic director, Ed "Moose" Krause stopped me at a spring football practice and asked me if I would be interested in meeting an old friend of his who was coming in to do a motivational film for a California-based business. His name was Pat O'Brien. Not the sportscaster of recent years, but a very famous movie star in the 1930s, 1940s, and 1950s. During his time, he was as famous as Robert De Niro and Sylvester Stallone.

I was really excited about meeting him! I have to tell you that way back when I was a little kid my mother used to give me a dime to go to the Saturday matinee at our local theater. O'Brien was one of my heroes, and now I was going to meet him!

One of O'Brien's most famous roles was starring as Knute Rockne, the legendary fighting Irish football coach whose teams established football fame for Notre Dame. The movie premiere was held in South Bend and featured another actor, Ronald Reagan, who played the part of George Gipp. Gipp was one of Rockne's most famous players who died of strep throat, a real killer in those days without our modern day antibiotics.

The story goes that when Gipp was so tragically ill, he told Rockne that some day when Notre Dame was losing and all odds were against them, to tell the guys, it's not too late – Go win one for the Gipper!" Rockne is said to have used this many times and the team did win one for the Gipper!

Upon meeting Pat O'Brien, I found him extremely personable and he seemed sincerely interested in my Saturday afternoon movie story about watching him. I asked him if he would have time to record a television interview with me while he was here. He told me to arrange what I wanted to do.

The Morris Inn is a very impressive hotel on the Notre Dame campus, so I chose that as the site for our interview. I positioned him on the patio at the inn with the Golden Dome prominently in view over his shoulder. As you know, the early and late news shows usually allow

only five or six minutes for their sports segments. But O'Brien was such a great interview that I did about twenty plus minutes with him! Throughout the week I used a portion of the interview five nights in a row. The interview was then showed in its entirety was used on a Saturday night program I did called "People in Sports".

When we concluded our visit, and after I thanked him, he expressed his appreciation for me inviting him. Then he said, "I'd like to offer to all of you who have been watching - my favorite old Irish Blessing –

May the wind be always at your back -
May your path always be downhill
May the sun always shine warm upon your face
May the rain always fall soft upon your fields
And may God always hold you and yours in the hollow of His hand."

My photographer and I sat there for several minutes absolutely transfixed by his words of the blessing – it was truly spellbinding.

I must tell you that after that day whenever I talked to service clubs, pep sessions, church groups, and others, the final words of my talk were to repeat this blessing and to always give credit to the great Pat

O'Brien.

RONALD REAGAN

On my initial trips to California when USC hosted Notre Dame in their lone series, I was almost awe struck visiting Los Angeles, the fabled home of movies and movie stars.

Like most people of the time, I had my favorite films – anything with John Wayne, James Cagney, Alan Ladd (of a great movie Shane) and others. But a film I somewhat accidentally saw was a movie called Kings Row. Ronald Reagan had a major part in the movie, and I remembered it because in one scene he ends up in a hospital for a minor ailment but the doctor puts him under anesthetic and amputates his legs. Reagan played this role very well. I never forgot that scene!

At the press party, held at the old and famous Ambassador Hotel at which we stayed (and which has long since been razed), a number of movie people mingled with others who were interested in the football game. I also met Scott Brady of the television series Shotgun Slade, his brother, Lawrence Tierney, Lee Marvin, and others, including Ronald Reagan.

I saw Reagan across the room and I walked over and introduced myself. I told him that I felt his performance in Kings Row was brilliant and I enjoyed the movie. We discussed Notre Dame football, the game, and I asked him about the Rockne movie. He complimented his co-star in the movie, Pat O'Brien.

As we continued to talk, Reagan informed me that he had been a baseball announcer for WHC, Des Moines, Iowa, during ticker tape recreations of Chicago Cubs games. He asked me if I had ever done a recreation, and fortunately I had. I explained my recreations were those of Notre Dame basketball games in New York and Buffalo when the broadcast expenses made doing it live a big cost loser. We talked about the techniques involved and he ventured his opinion that basketball must be very different and difficult because of pace!

When you do a ticker tape recreation, the paper coming out of the machine lists a player's number, field goal, personal foul, time of game, and score. You must know the players by the numbers. And you need a good imagination - in my case a great statistician and one who would be able to give you a quick break with a stats

report. You must have an engineer or producer who will run a pre-recorded audio tape of crowd noise and bring up the volume at the appropriate time to echo the announcer's excitement, i.e. when someone scores a basket.

Occasionally, the tape would stop and we would have to improvise a situation like water on the court being wiped up or a contact lens lost. One of the biggest compliments of my career came after doing a game one night, when Bill Starck and I stopped in a nearby sports bar for a drink and a sandwich. The people in the bar had been listening and wondered how we got back from New York so quickly. Our ticker tape broadcast was so strong that they thought we were doing it live!

There was something about Reagan which was very different and unusual. He had, for want of a better description, "an aura". His presence made you feel that you were the most important person in the room and that he had been waiting to talk to you. Several years later I was at a Young Republican National Convention in Omaha, Nebraska. Reagan was the headline speaker. There was a press conference held in the afternoon before his speech that night, and I went up to hear him answer questions. As I stood there, toward the back of the group, Reagan answered someone's question and

then looked at me and said, "Stay around when we finish." I waited around while his public relations man, Lyn Nofziger, cleared the room. Reagan came over and asked me if I was still the Notre Dame announcer and how were the prospects looking. He didn't remember my name, but he was able to identify me, and he still conveyed those same qualities – including the essence of making you feel important.

Years passed and Richard Nixon was nominated at the GOP National Convention in Miami. Reagan was a competitor but didn't get the nomination. The inside story, as I remember, was that he was closer to being the nominee than was the general information output by the press.

There are TV shows which many times ask the host or hostess to participate in a series of questions. Many times that question is, "Who do you admire and respect the most?" If and when I would ever be asked that question – my answer would be Ronald Reagan.

As an 85-year-old disabled veteran, a chaplain of my detachment for eight years, a member of the American Legion, and a member of the honor guard that was able to honor a deceased comrade with a twenty-one-gun salute, it is acceptable to opine that Reagan made me feel that America doesn't back down from countries who want to

attack us. He stood tall and was for America. Ronald Reagan was my hero.

HOAGY CARMICHAEL

There are memorable incidences in all of our lives that we wish we could preserve or record in some tangible way. The wonderful expression of "shoulda, woulda, coulda" seems to be alive and well forever.

A typical example of this occurred to me when I was working for the Indiana Department of tourism. That particular phase of my life was under the aegis of a dedicated and brilliant politician, lieutenant governor Dick Folz, from Evansville Indiana. He had provided new energy and ideas into what had preceded him- a stodgy department of tourism whose motto seem to be, "We've always done it this way. Why change?" One of governor Folz's truly revolutionary ideas was to explore and initiate more aggressive public relations activities.

I was assigned with one of his top assistants to work with ABC television in rendering any necessary help in their production of an outdoor series featuring celebrities like music icon Hoagy Carmichael, hosted by ABC sports announcer Chris Schenkel. Schenkel lives on a lake at Bippus, Indiana. I had met him several times during my Notre Dame sports career. So Chris and I renewed our acquaintanceship, and he knew, because of our past experience, that I would understand how and when and what to do to help.

Meeting Mr. Carmichael was an extremely pleasant experience. He was affable, gracious, and appreciative of our being there. He and Schenkel pre-recorded this program at Turkey Run State Park while fishing on Sugar Creek. During the production we really didn't have a great deal of important tasks for the ABC crew, but it was good that we were there to help solve some difficult situations if need be.

The program went well. Carmichael and Schenkel had an impressive chemistry between them, and I thought Chris did an outstanding job of hosting the program.

The final day arrived and the producer decided to have a late afternoon cookout. We were given the somewhat mundane assignment of gathering the preparations for the party – the hotdogs, hamburgers, buns, condiments, etc. The weather was perfect. It was an ideal setting for our wind-up picnic. It was in Indiana summer day when the heat and humidity stayed low.

Here's where I wish I had anticipated the events of the evening, but there would have been no way of doing that.

Hoagy regaled us with some funny and interesting stories of his movie and music career. It was fabulous, but I had no way to record it, even if he had given permission. Then at the end of our "gourmet" dining, he asked if we could get a piano outside so he could sing a little for all of us, if we wanted to hear a few songs. The piano arrived "seconds after his offer, because no one wanted him to change his mind.

The second magical moment began when I realized not only couldn't I record his stories but now what? Another lost opportunity. The great man held all of us spellbound as he sang "Stardust", "Old Buttermilk Sky", "Georgia on My Mind", and some of his other classics! It was a once-in-a-lifetime evening with the great native Hoosier, Hoagy Carmichael.

The man, a celebrity, whom we had all watch from afar, was a real down-to-earth person with no put ons! The night ended but the memories live on.

I think – I hope – you understand what I mentioned at the outset about the "shoulda, woulda, coulda" moments. The certain incidents we experience, which we can only remember – priceless moments which only rarely occur in our lifetime. I made a point of watching

the airing of the program when it was shown on ABC. It was outstanding and one of Schenkel's best!

MARCIA STARK

In the early 1970s, I worked for the Indiana Republican State Committee. This story begins with a new GOP state chairman bringing in his own people leaving many of us seeking other jobs.

The Marion County Republican chairman at that time was a brilliant politician, L. Keith Bulen. He had, a few years prior to this time, ousted a long-time GOP head man in Marion County by the name of Dale Brown. It was a major coup and subsequently he was the brilliant mentor behind long-time Indianapolis mayor, Richard Lugar, who was later elected as senator from Indiana. He also worked with another gifted and talented leader, Bill Hudnut. When Keith heard I was looking for a job, he offered me an opportunity with the Marion County GOP organization. I accepted since it was a perfect fit with my background and experience as a public relations person. I would schedule major Washington cabinet members, such as the Treasury Secretary and Secretary of Transportation, to campaign for various people running for Indiana state offices. It was a very challenging but rewarding position.

Since I needed a secretary and assistant, Keith assigned a volunteer aide named Marcia Stark to me. Marcia was bubbly, mentally sharp, and very dependable! She and I got along very well. The many details for preparation of advance work for these visiting officials included prompt time schedules, transportation in appropriate vehicles (with dependable drivers), press conferences, public appearances, radio interviews, and debates with the opposition. Also, something which may sound mundane to you, finding the location of restrooms!

At the time, I was returning to South Bend on Friday afternoons to still work Saturday radio on Notre Dame football games with co-announcer Van Patrick of the Mutual Radio Network.

One night Marcia and I were sitting in our office enjoying a late sandwich and a beer after a harrowing and trying couple of days. I told her what a great job she was doing and the invaluable help she was providing. I told her I would like to arrange for her and her parents to attend a Notre Dame home game. She deserved some appreciation for her dedication, and I wanted to reward her for her hard work in some way. I inquired what her father did for a living. She said he was a butcher. In South Bend at that time there were several custom meat markets, so I asked her if she or her parents had ever gone to a big time college football game at Notre Dame because the pre-game pageantry and the atmosphere is unforgettable. She said she would talk to them and let me know.

The next morning Keith called me into the office and laughed a little. He told me that Marcia and I were doing an excellent job. He was receiving a lot of compliments on our work. He told me it was very nice of me to invite Marcia and her parents to the "big time football game!" I told him that I felt she deserved it and since her father was a meat butcher he probably didn't get out much. I felt he would appreciate my invitation. "Well," Keith said, "did you ever hear of Stark and Wetzel Meats?" Of course I had, along with everyone else at the time, I knew the company was one of the biggest in the mid-west and their products were in supermarkets everywhere. Keith told me Marcia's father was a butcher, but he also owned Stark and Wetzels. I almost fell out of my chair. In addition, George Stark was a major recruiter for the University of Illinois! Marcia and I ended up laughing about my "big time" offer.

Marcia's parents became good friends, and George kidded me many times later about my offer. He was appreciative of my kind invitation, but never did get to South Bend for a home game. He did invite me to an Illinois game, but I never got there either.

DREWRYS BEER

A long-time television sponsor of some of my television sports programs was a local brewery, Drewrys Beer. You may or may not remember them with the Royal Canadian Mounted Policeman on their label. Along with the normal national brands like Miller, Budweiser, Falstaff, and Schlitz, there were other several minor brands, such as Champagne Velvet (CV) and Sterling, sold in South Bend and nearby states. However, these other minor brands were not sponsors of our telecasts, so Bill and I became associated with Drewrys.

It was always interesting to me that when I went out after the late TV sports show or games with Bill Starck, people would volunteer that they couldn't stand to drink Drewrys – that it always caused them (to be polite) "problems" the next day. They would tell us things like, "Drewrys gives me headaches and 'problems'. It's a CV for me!"

During the period just before the Notre Dame football seasons, several of our sponsors would ask me to talk to their sales associates and other employees. Drewrys always invited me to address their workers in a wonderfully equipped bar with deli food and ice-cold draft beer. I always enjoyed going there and performing because the people were just great! The food and drinks likewise.

The first time I was there, they invited me to take a tour of the brewery at the conclusion of the meeting. We went in the area where the cans and bottles were filled and it was very interesting to see how smoothly the pallets of product moved to be filled.

Then a surprise – the Drewrys' line stopped. Bottles, cans, and new pallets of Champagne Velvet rolled out to be filled. Then next came Sterling beer cans and bottles. THE VERY SAME BEER IN DIFFERENT CONTAINERS!!!

And until this day, I never divulged this "secret!"

***It should be noted that recently both the Champagne Velvet and Sterling brands were relaunched and are not bottled this way today.**

DAVE MCINTIRE

One of my most successful endeavors and associations was a marriage of my TV and radio commercial experience and success was with a very prominent Chevrolet dealer in Indy.

I met Dave McIntire through some mutual acquaintances who were sports fans and knew of my background at Notre Dame. McIntire had recently moved from a Chevrolet store in Bloomington, Indiana, and there was an opening to do his radio/TV advertising. He did his own newspaper ads but was open on the electronic media. In contrast to most dealers at that time and even now, he had no desire to be his own TV or radio spokesperson. How very different! We immediately developed a rapport and found we had common interests. I referred him to Van Gates Chevrolet in South Bend, my long time TV sports sponsor, for endorsements and recommendations of my work.

His dealership at that time was located in a fairly modest and small location – far from "Automobile Row" – that expression referring a variety of car dealerships located in close proximity to each other. However, he was in the process to begin building a large deluxe Chevy store on "the row" which would be large enough to accommodate five hundred or more cars and trucks in inventory.

We started by doing some orthodox, run of the mill type of radio/TV ads. Then, prior to the opening of his new location and state-of-the-art building, I proposed a series of rather different commercials with a novel appeal. For example, for the grand opening I had a one-minute spot with people getting on a small plane and a shot of customers "dropping" in for the great buys! "At Dave McIntire's Chevrolet Center at 5161 W. 38th Street." That was all the audio, and of course we superimposed only the new address. I used a public access piece of music and that was it.

Another commercial had people in various dress – wedding costumes, ballet dresses, little children with parents, clowns, football, basketball, and baseball players, farmers, and 500 racers, all coming into the dealership from different directions. "Everybody from everywhere is coming to McIntire's Chevrolet Center."

Again we used no audio for most of the commercial, except at the end – just music!

We even did a spot on service. We started the video with a couple looking at a service bill and screaming about the high cost being much more than the estimate. Then the same couple at Dave McIntire's counting their money "literally" in savings. We ended with some testimony from satisfied new car buyers.

At the end of that campaign, I brought in Paul Hornung from Louisville, Kentucky, to do some spots. Paul had won the Heisman trophy at Notre Dame and the Super Bowl with the Green Bay Packers. McIntire gave him a new Corvette to use periodically as compensation.

During an economic down-turn and shortly after the new location opened, the Hornung campaign and others were an immediate success. Of course sharing the credit for the booming sales at the Chevrolet Center was an outstanding sales force which was very customer oriented under the brilliant direction of Dave McIntire. It also was very rewarding to me and the TV/Radio advertising campaign! Mr. McIntire paid a great deal of credit for the store's extraordinary sales to the advertising strategy! He told me several times over the years we spent together "that the measure of advertising, if it is successful, is that they will come!"

And I am proud to say I had a part in this once great dealership which not only was a sales leader in Indiana, but one of the top dealerships in the country!

Our association concluded when I had an offer to go into a business as an ownership partner with a friend who capitalized a company named "Video Shack". My investment was small, but I received a substantial stock portion based upon my advertising expertise. We ran the business into a store chain – two stores in South Bend, four in Indy, and one in Bloomington.

This was also a very successful venture. I thought it would justify the hard work and sacrifices I had made and it was going well until I discovered more was going out in monies to my partner than we had coming in.

I have always believed people and trusted them, which was a big mistake in this instance. But tough lessons are learned sometimes – this was one! However, because of my experience with quality people like Dave McIntire and countless others over the years, I do still look for and expect the best out of my fellow man.

BIG BROTHERS

There are times in our lives when the timing is right and you are given the opportunity to give back to people or organizations.

It was when I was handling the radio and television advertising for Dave McIntire's Chevrolet Center in Indianapolis that one such opportunity was afforded to me.

Mr. McIntire was on the board of directors of the Indianapolis Big Brothers. One day when we were planning an advertising project, he told me that United Way had made severe cuts in Big Brothers funding and the group needed to discover ways to make up the short fall. The situation required some urgent and immediate solutions.

He asked me to give it some thought and to attend an upcoming board meeting with him where I could offer my recommendations for solving the financial problem. I

had been President of the St. Joseph County Cancer Society and helped in fund raising projects for the South Bend Kiwanis Club, so I did have some experience in this area.

Several very orthodox ideas were discussed at the meeting but I proposed something radically different to the board. My suggestion was to hold an annual dinner with special "big-name" sports celebrities as guest speakers. I told them the dinner should be limited to a targeted, wealthier audience so that they could make the tickets expensive, raffle off some big-time prizes, and give everyone a significant table gift.

The board members liked my ideas and asked me if I would help to develop it further. I was asked to get the initial speakers. Several were a little skeptical about the possibility of getting some truly "big names" for the first dinner, so I told them I would get two famous celebrities that would please everyone. How about Paul Horning, the Notre Dame All-American Quarterback, Heisman trophy winner and star halfback with the NFL Super Bowl champion Green Bay Packers? And how about ABC television's number one sports announcer, Chris Schenkel? I invited them and they were the stars at our first dinner which was held at the Indianapolis Athletic Club.

I asked the speakers to talk for about ten minutes and then do a question and answer session which was enthusiastically received. The speaker honorarium I set at $2,500. A very modest amount for them and included a first class plane ticket. However, being the men of character that they are, both Hornung and Schenkel donated their honorariums back to Big Brothers. And neither used the plane ticket. Hornung drove in from Louisville, Kentucky, where he lived. Schenkel flew in from New York in his private plane.We priced the tickets at $200.00 each and we sold out with our limit of 200 attendees. Everyone had to buy a ticket. There were to be no free passes. The top prize at that dinner was $5,000 in cash, second prize was $3,000 and third was $2,000 cash.

We arranged for an Indianapolis policeman to accompany each winner home. We raffled off some significant gifts such as his and her golf sets, his and her bicycles, a cruise, and other impressive prizes. As a table favor, everyone received a high quality Swiss army knife. An open bar was also a unique part of the evening. Dave McIntire and the board members were overwhelmed with the dinner's success and the amount of money raised. The only negative was a board member who emceed the dinner envisioning himself as a star attraction. He talked too much and told lengthy, unfunny jokes- I think you get the picture. For the next seven years that I produced and staged the dinner, I assigned myself as the MC to ensure no more problems with a self-styled, want-to-be comedian.

In subsequent dinners, I brought in Howard Cosell of ABC Sports and Monday Night Football whose first words were, "Is the press going to be here?" I told him, "No. Everything is off the record." He said, "Great! Get me a couple of double martinis as soon as you can." He was one of the most cooperative, friendly and engaging people I have ever met!

Paul Hornung and I had developed a bit of a relationship over the years not only because of our Notre Dame connection, but also because of the commercial work I was able to get for him with McIntire Chevrolet. Nowadays it seems as if every athlete is a spokesperson for something, but back then this wasn't the case. Not only did this relationship help with Paul being our first speaker, but I was very fortunate in getting Paul to help me in obtaining Cosell's Monday Night football partners, Don Meredith and hall of famer, Frank Gifford. Meredith was also the star of a very popular TV program, Police Story. Both Gifford and Meredith were outstanding in every way.

Many people forget Meredith was an outstanding quarterback for several years for the Dallas Cowboys. He was the Dallas QB in the famous Green Bay/Dallas "Ice Bowl" playoff game! He was one of the very best we ever had. Hornung, who returned frequently to the event, and Dandy Don enjoyed Chardonnay wine extensively the night that Meredith was the special guest. Don had been told by Cosell that our dinner was a relaxing and fun event. And this night, probably with help from the wine, Don was feeling very relaxed which led to quite a humorous story that he shared.

During the Meredith Q & A, someone asked Meredith about his co-star, the beautiful, striking blonde actress, Angie Dickinson. Dandy Don described her as an outstanding professional and very hard working. He then related an incident that happened during one of their programs when everything was going wrong. They were doing this one scene over and over, until finally the director said, "Let's take a fifteen-minute break, and we will try it one more time today."

In the scene, Meredith, whose character was a detective named Dirk, had been shot and was lying in a hospital bed. His partner, Dickinson, was to enter into his room, come over to his bedside, and say some lines of encouragement. But both she and he kept missing the

words and the timing. Meredith had set the picture for the dinner audience and when let us know the cast and crew finished their break and proceeded to set up to try it one last time. The director said, "Action," and Dickinson came up to his bedside, leaned over, and said in a very loud voice, "Dirk, if you get well damn soon I am going to ---- your brains out!" Everyone at the dinner broke up. At this moment, Don realized what he had said, and where he had said. He turned to our regular priest who was there for the invocation and benediction, slightly embarrassed, and said to him, "Father forgive me, please!" Our priest simply smiled and said, "I have heard worse, Don."

The third member of that famous Monday Night Football telecast team was the distinguished and extremely impressive Hall of Famer, Frank Gifford, who had been an All-American halfback at Southern California and a New York Giant icon.

When I contacted Gifford, whom I had the honor of meeting and interviewing a few years earlier when I was the sports voice at Notre Dame, he accepted my invitation to be that year's speaker immediately after checking the date. I explained about our honorarium and the plane ticket and out-of-pocket allowance for other expenses. Gifford said, "Forget it. I have a friend who will fly me in that night in his private jet, and I'll stay as long as you want and do whatever you want for the program." Frank Gifford has his own personality. He was not only an accomplished athlete, but he had finesse and savoir faire. He mingled with the guests very well. Everyone was so very impressed with his answers to a myriad of questions, the length of time he stayed, and his extreme courtesy in posing with our dinner guests for individual pictures. Everyone came away from the event thinking what a wonderful guy this man is. Frank Gifford was not only a gifted athlete and broadcaster but the epitome of a gentlemen's gentleman as well.

Others who spoke at the Big Brother dinner included Dick Butkus of the Chicago Bears, Olympic decathlon champion, Bob Mathias, who won the gold medal at the age of seventeen, Jimmy the Greek, and Earl Morrall. Morrall is famous as the backup quarterback for several teams, most notably, the Miami Dolphins. The Dolphins at that time were coached by Don Shula, Morrall's former coach when they were both with the Baltimore Colts. Earl proved a substantial asset when he substituted for an injured Bob Griese in eleven games in 1972. The Dolphins were, and still are, the only unbeaten NFL championship team to go an entire season without a loss, which would not have been possible without Morrall's contributions. As a result, Earl was named the

AFC player of the year and won the NFL's inaugural Comeback Player of the Year in 1972.

The Big Brothers experience gave me the opportunity to give back. I feel the Lord put me in that challenging position to provide help for the Big Brother organization and the many kids it serves.

INDIANAPOLIS 500 and MR. HULMAN

One summer when I found out the Indianapolis Motor Speedway Museum had been completed, our chief photographer, Chuck Linister, who was a very talented individual who helped me make reality out of some of the off-beat ideas of mine, and I went to Indianapolis for some interviews. My Bardohl man, Sherm Searer, flew us to Indianapolis so I could do the interview and not miss my daily TV and radio sports programs.

The man I had arranged to interview, with the help of their public relations director, was the owner of the speedway, Tony Hulman.

He was waiting for us and took us first around the museum to show off its collection of vintage cars. It was a magnificent display of the early winners to the contemporary machines. The builders had not finished with positioning the lighting so Chuck was having a

problem with one position on the floor. We asked Mr. Hulman if we could move a car or two so they would be more properly shown. Not only did this gracious and considerate gentleman tell us, "Yes, whatever you need to do," but he took off his suit coat and helped us move the cars for the right lighting.

I interviewed Mr. Hulman subsequently many more times and was always was impressed with this humble, self-effacing man who preserved the 500 Speedway and all the grand traditions that go with the race which made Indiana famous around the world. I will never forget this icon and his willingness to help us do it right.

Over the years, the speeds at the Indianapolis Motor Speedway have increased at every race. But once there was a 160 average speed barrier that couldn't be broken until a race icon by the name of Parnelli Jones did it on a qualification day, and I was there to do interview. I was near his garage when he returned right after setting that record and I asked him if he would talk to me. A horde of television, radio, and newspaper reporters moved in and more or less crowded me out of my position. They called out to him with questions, but he said, "Wait a minute! This man was first," and he motioned to me to come over. Parnelli was considerate of me and certainly could have passed on my interview and

talked to the Chicago, New York, or other "big timers", but he didn't. He later won the 500 and we talked in later years about his courtesy.

A few years later when I was the week-end sports announcer at WLW-1 Channel 13, Indianapolis, ABC arranged to telecast the race. This was the year the famous Chris Schenkel would be the TV anchor! The producers at ABC came to the station and offered us an opportunity to be track reporters.

I volunteered to work Turn #1. Race day came – nothing, absolutely nothing happened on Turn #1. Every bit of action took place on Turns #3 and #4. Standing next to me most of the day was Hollywood movie star, Jim Garner. He had a silver race credential which allowed him access anywhere. We spent most of the race on Turn #1 listening to Sid Collins on the radio coverage. My highlight period consisted mostly standard of comments about what I saw and a quick interview of the Maverick TV star.

However, this was a memorable event for me because an Indianapolis car dealer was selected to drive the pace car with Schenkel as his passenger so he could report on the start of the race. As the "driver" left the track after pacing for a few laps, he left at too high a speed and crashed into some bleachers. Fortunately, no

one was injured, but from then on, the pace car driver's qualifications changed!

DR. McGONIGLE

One of several bittersweet experiences in my life took place when I worked at a video franchise company based in Malibu, California. I was hired to manage a "pilot store" to illustrate what a franchise store should look like. I was to travel with the company's CEO and make presentations of the video franchise opportunities. I was also to present some other details such as build out costs, how to set up proper displays, and how to prepare ads for print, radio, and television.

It was an excellent position for me with my background! Jodie and I found an apartment almost across the street (albeit shoe box in size), but right on the beach! It was truly an idyllic situation. We both were grateful to the good Lord above for it all. After about a month on the job, it could not have been better.

One Sunday morning I picked up a bottle of

champagne – not the ordinary Andre – but Mumms, WOW! Big time! And a couple of plastic champagne flutes.

I had hired some people to work the store when I was not available, and this Sunday I was off – taking some time to prepare for a trip to Boston, New York, and Philadelphia.

Jodie and I went down to the beach to have some champagne and to toast to our good fortune. Sunday morning the beach was devoid of people – just she and I walking. I was standing with my back to the ocean and, BOOM, it happened. Jodie yelled at me to move further up towards her, but too late, a gigantic wave had come out of nowhere. It knocked me down, and as I tried to crawl out of the water, the riptide kept taking me back out! I had been SCUBA certified for a long time, but believe me it didn't do any good at this moment. I thought, "This is a hell of a way to go." The riptide continuously kept pulling me back into the water. I was attempting to crawl out of the water, bending my fingernail all the way back in the process and, more severely, injuring my knee. Jodie was unable to help since she couldn't swim, but it didn't matter anyway because she thought I was playing around. She kept saying, "Don't be funny. Don't be funny!" I thought, "Funny? What do you think is I'm doing?"

Finally, I was able to crawl up onto the beach.

I was out of the water, but not out of trouble. My knee blew up immediately, swelling to almost volleyball size. Of course, after the panic from the near drowning had subsided, I decided that I would just have to tough this out for awhile. Jodie got some drugstore crutches. I hobbled across the street to the video franchise headquarters where I worked. With my "know-it-all" attitude, I just knew it was simply a severe sprain which would be fine in a few days.

I was obviously wrong and the swelling did not go down, in fact it worsened.

A lady in our apartment complex had seen me hobbling around and suggested I see a doctor. She referred me to her doctor who had done a very successful surgery on her back. We called and made an appointment with her physician, a Dr. McGonigle in nearby Santa Monica.

When we arrived, we were shown to a typical medical examination room, except it wasn't typical at all. The walls were full of Notre Dame campus pictures!

Dr. John McGonigle was a strikingly handsome man in an Armani suit who had a bedside manner which immediately put me at ease. I asked him about the Notre Dame pictures and about his interest in South Bend. We were very surprised when he told us he was on the Board of Trustees at the University and frequently went back to trustee meetings in South Bend. He was equally surprised about my background as the radio and television play-by-play announcer of Notre Dame football/basketball for 15+ years. We had attended the same football practices over the years and never met until my knee injury in California.

Subsequently, he informed me the wave had torn my anterior and media collateral cruciate ligaments and damaged the cartilage beyond repair.

We became friends while I underwent surgery and rehab.

A reminder to all – it is, indeed, a small, small, world!

THE DR. O'CONNOR QUESTION

There is another interesting "adventure" connecting my career at Notre Dame radio and television to a doctor that was treating me.

I had undergone colon cancer surgery at Hancock Regional Hospital. The day after the operation, I began having major problems in breathing – so serious that they rushed me "STAT" up to intensive care for emergency treatment. I was alert enough to recognize a roomful of nurses and two doctors, one of whom was a Notre Dame graduate, a Dr. O'Connor. Here I must interject that my wife, Jodie, when it started to look very grim, had called a man I worked with, Maury Mayfield and his wife, and they came to the hospital to be with her.

I had been fitted with a full face mask but I was still progressively struggling to breathe. Maury stood on one side of my bed and Dr. O'Connor opposite. As I lay there,

the mask hindering, not helping, my breathing, Maury said to Dr. O'Connor, "You better take good care of this guy. He is one of yours, a Notre Damer. He used to announce the Notre Dame football games."

O'Connor then said, "Oh, no! He can't be!"

Maury replied, "Oh, yes he is!"

In the meantime, I was desperately trying to breathe. Maury then said, "Ask him something about Notre Dame football".

O'Connor said, "If he is who you say he is, (Keep in mind I'm listening to this dialogue and still trying to breathe under the full face mask which was not helping at all!) then who made the legendary tackle in the game against Oklahoma in Notre Dame stadium?"

I knew the answer, thank goodness. I told them, through the mask, that Dan Shannon tackled Sooner half-back Buddy Leake so hard that Leake fumbled and had to leave the game. The play, which happened on the kick-off to begin the contest, set the stage for an Irish upset victory.

O'Connor said to Maury, "He is right. Shannon is my nephew!"

After this "monumental debate" about this unforgettable game and Shannon's play, they finally got my breathing normalized under the direction of Dr.

O'Connor.

I just wonder what would have occurred if I had not known the answer?

MY FINAL THOUGHTS

These are some final thoughts I have now as I receive dialysis treatments three or four days a week.

Hearing about the passing of the great "Gentlemen's Gentleman", Hall of Fame football player, and member of the original Monday Night Football crew, Frank Gifford, hit me pretty hard. It reminded me once again of our mortality. Howard Cosell and Don Meridith, his co-hosts, passed years earlier. As you read, all had appeared for me when I chaired and produced the first series of Indianapolis Big Brothers fund raising dinners in the 70's.

Inexorably, time moves on. Some other things I want to say because of the people – their names are simply listed in the acknowledgment section, but I want to write a line or two about some of them.

My wife, Jodie, is at the top of the list in my mind because of her giving through some very difficult health

issues and crises in recent years. The Lord blessed me with this wonderful partner.

When I was close in succumbing to a rare e-coli infection, a doctor, Michael Fletcher, the Chief of Staff at Hancock Regional Hospital, took over treatment and saved my life. Since then he has become a good friend as well. (It helped that he is a Notre Damer!) And thanks to his daughter, Katie, who brought sunshine into my hospital room when it was almost overcome with clouds.

Jim and Patti Cole have been always there to aid and comfort Jodie during several of my hospital emergencies. I particularly refer to a crisis when I nearly bled to death at two in the morning. Jodie called them and they simply asked, "Where?" They drove from Shelbyville, Indiana, to I.U. Medical emergency room to be with her in Indianapolis. True friends!

We also have been truly blessed by the good Lord

who has allowed us to know Jim and Linda Grabowski, devout Christians who epitomize practicing Christian ideals. Linda has shepherded Jodie many times, while Jim, although much younger than me, has been a mentor to me in many ways. These two deserve recognition for having gone so far above and beyond for Jodie and me that there are no words in my vocabulary to adequately express our gratitude.

Pastor John Davis and his perfect partner, Stacy, represent the epitome of a Disciple of Christ. John's memorable gifts of his time to be with us are too many to recite.

Thanks to Valarie Nickelson and Mary Ann Martin for their encouragement and also to the people at Fresenius Dialysis Center who have kept, and are keeping, me alive with their outstanding and cheerful treatments. They include Dr. John Lucia, manager Jeff, nurses Mandy and Christine, techs Brandy, Brittanie, Marie, and Meghan, and many many others.

Our grandson, Ryan Coghill, an educator, assistant school principal by vocation, and his gracious wife, Lesley, have so many times reminded me that family is so very important! The encouragement from his mother and father, Mike and Brenda Coghill, has been special, as have the Bercks, Jodie's sister-in-law and her family, who

have always made me feel a welcome member of the family.

The widow of my "Brother Bill", Patti Starck, has, since Bill's passing six years ago, continued to include Jodie and me as part of that family's private celebrations and occasions. Those many thoughtful enclosures are forever indelibly imprinted in my mind and memory.

I shall not test your patience much further in offering these personal remembrances of wonderful people who have played a major role in my life. There are no adequate words in my vocabulary to convey my appreciation, so I simply say thanks to all of you!!

I have already told you about my interview with the great actor, Pat O'Brien, and his introduction to me of that old Irish Blessing. It is a line from that blessing that I have held dear in my heart for so many years- to all of you:

"MAY GOD ALWAYS HOLD YOU AND YOURS IN THE HOLLOW OF HIS HAND!

ACKNOWLEDGEMENTS

I have had many people in my life who have contributed in so many ways to my character, my career and my life.

To begin, I thank Foster Fudge and A.G. Vance for hiring me in my first professional position as a sports announcer at WFMU, Crawfordsville, Indiana, when I was a freshman at Wabash College - “professional” meaning I got paid- they were the owners of the Crawfordsville Journal-Review newspaper and WFMU.

I owe thanks to Frank Crosiar, General Manager of WHOT in South Bend, who hired me right after I left the military when I urgently needed a job.

I must acknowledge the incomparable Notre Dame football coach, Ara Parseghian, from whom I learned a lot about football and character. His handling and interaction with people, along with his discipline and determination were just some of the many reasons he is a talented and successful man. I was always very appreciative of his help when we were together on our Sunday Notre Dame Game Hi-Lights program.

Bernie Barth, WNDU-TV, who gave me the opportunity to try out for the sports director job – it was what I had worked for and prayed for – and he took me with no TV experience, having confidence that I would be a quick learner, and I was. To this wonderful man who has passed, I owe so very much, and I will never forget the precious gift he gave to me – 15 plus years covering Notre Dame sports on radio and television.

I am grateful to Tom Hamilton and Bazil O'Hagan for the flexibility to allow the resources to expand my sports coverage under their general management tenures; our radio managers, ex-marine, Dan Martin and Bob Nowicki, who also gave me the support I needed many times.

I would also like to thank my color commentators on the Notre Dame football and basketball telecasts: former assistant football coach under the great Frank Leahy, Bill Earley, who was the finest color commentator I ever heard; former Irish and Detroit Lion half back "Chick" Magcioli; Irish quarterback, the great Frank

Tripucka.

I also wish to thank the sports publicity directors at Notre Dame, Charlie Callahan and Roger Valdiseari whose talents were without equal in their positions.

I save these thankful words for a one and only Ed "Moose" Krause. There will never be anyone like this beloved Notre Dame athletic director of many years. Ed "Moose" Krause was a man who gave so much to so many!

Another facet of my life was in politics. I was active as a young Republican in St. Joseph County. I worked in several local campaigns. I worked for the Indiana Republican State Committee – my mentor was St. Joseph County Republican Chairman, Perley Provest, an ex-marine whose political acumen was unequaled. Perley and his wife, Ellie, also served as a stabilizing effect on me during some challenging personal times. Through him I had the honor of knowing the CEO of Associates Company, Mike Carmichael, and other prominent GOP figures. Perley was responsible for my acceptance of the position of Public Relations and Director of Communications for the GOP State Committee.

True highlights of my life in Indianapolis and Greenfield were to be a member of the Greenfield American Legion Honor Guard. and also serving on the

Greenfield Veterans' Memorial Committee. My thanks for the privilege go to ex-marine, Bob Workman and former Greenfield Mayor, Brad Dereamer.

I was also honored by being voted as a member of a select group of honorary associate members of Marine Corps League Detachment 1253 in Morristown, Indiana, and one of my proudest achievements was to serve as chaplain for eight years.

Perley Provost III, his wife Renee, and their family in South Bend are others I wish to thank for many acts of kindness.

I could thank many others of you but space is a problem.

I always have enjoyed the Warner Brothers cartoons which ended with Porky Pig saying
"eh-eh- That's all folks!" I wish to echo his words by saying to you, "That's all folks! And thank you for reading my book." It's late in the fourth quarter for me and the clock is running.

When I signed off on my sportscasts or sporting events, my sign-off words were, "Good night and good sports" – and that's how I leave you here, "Good night and good sports!"

GO IRISH!!!

CREDITS

My writing of this book would not have been possible without the endless patience, typing, and re-typing of Carole Robison. She has become a dear friend. Also, to her husband, Larry, a thanks as well for his contributions of proofing the book. Don't worry, the Cubs will come back next year! As Rush Limbaugh's fans often say, "Ditto," to Nancy Porter

To Tony Sturgeon, what can I say about the editing expertise and overall directions your provided, along with the huge amount of your time. You are the recipient of many thanks, compliments and all the words of appreciation I'm able to convey! Your time is the most precious gift of all because time can never be replaced.

Often people who make frequent speeches (many times too long) use the words "and finally" and then go on for eons, or the words, "I will conclude", and then go on to use the word "summarize" and then hopefully END!

So, please permit me to credit one more individual, my wife, Jodie. She suggested many times that I should write this book. She had patience when she caught me up at 2:00 or 3:00 AM writing, and after a "brief" lecture about me needing my rest, gave me significant and, many times, necessary words of encouragement!

51822189R00077

Made in the USA
Charleston, SC
04 February 2016